Restland

poems by

Nicholas Barnes

Finishing Line Press
Georgetown, Kentucky

Restland

For Walt Whitman, Dr. Bill Gholson, and Reilly Nycum

Acknowledgments

Grateful acknowledgment is made to the following publications, in which these poems originally appeared, sometimes in different forms:

a child said, what is the grass? [in *Divot: A Journal of Poetry*]
poem at five [in *BEATIFIC*]
little cole [in *oddball magazine*]
yolanda [in *Bear Creek Gazette*]
rambling drive [in *300 Days of Sun*]
june watches ballgames in heaven [in *Pamplemousse*]
bullpen and highway 62 [in *Juste Milieu*]
painting hands [in *Cola Literary Review*]
gone fishing and poet kills bird [in *The Ana*]
eighth grade funeral [in *The Phoenix*]
ashes [in *Progenitor Art & Literary Journal*]
until next time, buddy [in *Sage Cigarettes*]
maison de rêve and static and damaged parts, no warranty [in *Misfit Magazine*]
oakland 2011 [in *Meniscus*]
gaggle [in *Chinchilla Lit*]
armistice [in *Mixed Mag*]
lament [in *The Bluebird Word*]
don't take my word for it [bad advice] [in *trampset*]
s.o.s. [in *Open Minds Quarterly*]
a sudden shift in glasnost [in *RockPaperPoem*]
j. dean boys and fairy tale [in *BRUISER*]
awaken [in *Spit Poet Zine*]
i wrote your name at the top of the neues rathaus [in *Fish Barrel Review*]
beach street [in *NonBinary Review*]
we held hands [in *Eclectica Magazine*]
better med [in *Barzakh*]
roll on tanner creek [in *O:JA&L; Open: Journal of Arts & Letters*]
now i know why tom & huck staged their own funerals [in *Gold Man Review*]
au revoir [in *Scapegoat Review*]

Publisher: Leah Huete de Maines
Editor: Christen Kincaid
Cover Art: Reilly Rachel Nycum
Author Photo: Reilly Rachel Nycum
Cover Design: Elizabeth Maines McCleavy

Order online: www.finishinglinepress.com
also available on amazon.com

Author inquiries and mail orders:
Finishing Line Press
PO Box 1626
Georgetown, Kentucky 40324
USA

Contents

a child said, what is the grass?

it's your bully waiting for you
in the bathroom at lunchtime.

> it's waking up from your chronic nightmares
> only to find you're in sleep paralysis.

it's having recess basketballs thrown at your head—
they didn't want to play with you anymore.

> it's an eighth grade hairline ankle fracture—
> you didn't want to join that football team.

it's seeing both of your great grandmothers
before, during, and after that dementia.

> it's being told that you're fat
> and not knowing how to stand up for yourself.

it's getting called a pussy by your coach
even though you're trying your best.

> it's getting made fun of
> for going vegetarian in high school.

it's a vacation gone wrong—
you had a nervous breakdown in seattle.

> it's a breakup in a sophomore dorm room—
> you built up a wall, brick by brick.

it's alcoholism inherited—
it's mental illness manifested.

> it's spending every day trying to forget the trinity—
> the emotional, verbal, and holy physical.

it's an attempt to lock pain away in poems
even though there's not enough paper in the world to do that.

poem at five

look, look at how
the mimosa tree
sheds its skin
upon his own,
just like snowflakes.

gaze, gaze upon
the railroad ties
that encircle
the vegetables, soil,
and leaning flowers.
walking between the raised rows,
a boy once stood lost in his garden.

growing,
set eyes upon how we grow,
just like the green beans
and tomatoes do
in the dirt where his feet
are planted deep,
like roots.

watch, watch him grieve
as the summer slowly ends.
autumn sets in,
and that sweet essence leaves
those dying branches and trees.

thoughts of the fruitless garden
race through his mind.
the young boy waits to see
what he will plant
in seasons to come.

little cole

adored the wizard of oz, and for his birthday one year, he was gifted dorothy, tin man, scarecrow, and lion barbie dolls. they were soon replaced with g.i. joe action figures. little cole wanted to be just like peter pan. he believed if he could muster enough happy thoughts, he might be able to lift off too. but ultimately, he blamed his flightless, grounded bones on a lack of fairy dust. little cole was taken on hunting trips. the animals he saw were magnificent, but eventually became riddled with cold steel bullets. he pictured himself as a photographer shooting the land instead of the furry creatures. little cole put on his mother's clothes once or twice before it was deemed off limits. he felt great, he felt alive, he felt he was someone he'd never met before. little cole in college supposed it was a revelation the first time he saw drag. he was living through those queens, like they were in touch with the secrets of the universe. little cole saw a beautiful stranger when he finally summoned the courage to wear makeup. he realized that with just a bit of mascara, lipstick, nail polish, and maybe a bit of jewelry, you could fashion yourself a brand new boy in a matter of minutes. little cole now feels he may be a cactus flower that will only blossom at night. his thorns soften and his petals open when no one's watching. at least these days, he knows who he really is at heart.

yolanda

swing set scene, sawdust mulch,
pea gravel, metal clip ringing
against the flagpole.
dead grass, outdoor breezeway,
baseball diamond with daisies
poking out.
debra the recess lady.
wooden silhouettes lining the
chain link fence.
creamsicle clownfish with apricot
and snow white stripes.
post-assembly box of
snickerdoodle sugar cookies.
flimsy, awkward, wrinkled
plastic gloves.
a stop light, a lunchroom traffic
signal with red, green, and
yellow.
milk cartons that would never
open right.
a hostile little monkey bar gang.
four square kids, tetherball kids,
soccer and basketball cliques.
tiny beanie babies, glossy
posters, ridiculously large
pencils, fruity candy and
markers.
a librarian that smelled like
pennies, an art teacher from
latvia, cafeteria girls on a smoke
break.
students pretending they didn't
see.
collective punishment, on the
wall during playtime, a kid that
didn't fess up.
rainbow parachute, classmates
under the colorful canopy,
alone together.
a kid without friends, a kid
crying in class, a kid who'd
rather be anywhere else.

rambling drive

grandpa stan
used to keep
a floral porcelain
coffee cup on the dash
of his chevy truck.

when i rode with him,
his charming 12v lighter
captured my imagination
and my finger once when
i pulled back the spring:
yeah i gave my pointer a
coil-shaped branding.
i was the kid constantly
fascinated by fire.

next thing i remember was
fridge cold aloe vera—
drugstore neon slickery gel
didn't stop screaming pain,
made it more of a dull shout.

he al[so]ways had those
curiously strong peppermints
that looked like huge old pills.
now i keep my guitar picks
in an altoid's tin like his.
had it so long it's starting to rust,
just like he has by now.

and days like this i think of him
and his bing crosby voice,
and all those sights + sounds,

like perfumed boxwood shrubs
outside his big white house,
the sandy soil, best tomatoes,
powdery yellow plums
on the cool green grass,
and that carton of

misty 2000s
he let me buy
for grandma aggie
at the albertsons.

june watches ballgames in heaven

you used to watch cubs games
from your living room.
wearing your pinstripe jersey
with the big red c for chicago.
you and your trusty pup, sosa,
would cheer for every run.
 then you fell sick.
you'd spend your time sitting
at the kitchen table instead.
filling out coloring books,
playing gin rummy.
you forgot my name.
you became a stranger.
 after you left, i remember
seeing you in that casket.
the light was from a movie.
it hit your face like a starlet.
like peggy lee, like doris day.
and i said goodbye.
 for the past fifteen years,
i've been calling collect.
i never really got through.
but on those rare nights,
i saw you, smiling.
you knew my name again.

bullpen

your graphite skin
reminds me of blood
dripping by the pint
onto brittle paper leaves
and pink silken blossoms.

turning dead hues deader,
i fortified them with iron,
all because my brother hurled
that baseball across the yard,
catching my left brow unawares.

a wineskin with a thorn in its side,
innocence flowed through tiny hands
trying to shield stinging eyes
from monochrome bees imagined
who trade blue day for pitch night.

in the after hours doc's office
they sewed up my stitches,
which later fell off like a curve,
clipped out of my forehead:
kitchen scissors and isopropyl.

painting hands

brushing my scar shaped like new hampshire. i could never get the contours. never right, the wrinkly dimples. somewhere between concord and keene i lost the slender lowercase d outline. so instead i resigned my hands to the dirt with the band-aid worms. wedding ringed around number four. hands on homecomely hips. one pair of hands lifts the ax. the other holds the log. to the knuckle, she said. a horse bit off her dad's finger. a rat tore mine, my pinky it bled. brother barnes died splitting wood for his l.d.s. ward. hands on heart, clenching shirt scruffs. trying to warm hands for winter. lacquered hands hanging on hooks. jesused hands missing new england. signing for hangfire salvation. hands on the mat. hands too weak to break free. hands seldom raised victorious. glove on the left. ball in the right. a grounder opened my fingernail like a tuna can. hands in splints. a childhood in bandages. a childhood that should've been spent playing cowboy. a cap gun drifter, keeping the peace in the backyard. i thought about death from an early age; hands on the serrated metal belly. hands in pockets, approaching another casket. where do cowboys go when they die? boot hill. until god comes along, paints their portrait, and puts them up in heaven's waiting room. until their hands turn to castilleja colored feathers in the highest.

gone fishing

he sat and waited on the umpqua riverbank. basking in the sun with two ice-cold sixpacks.

walking across the river bottom, straddling the slippery bedrock, i peeked into the submerged fissure: fifteen or more bass shadows zigzagging, hiding from the swift current.

dipping my pole into that water, teasing my electric blue lure, i watched the tip of the shakespeare rod until i felt the hook set.

reeling in, my eyes beheld a glistening, twitching smallmouth. gasping for air, crying out for something to drink. hanging off the end of my thin nylon string.

forgot the billy club. no sticks or stones in sight.

he held the slimy submarine toward me, facefirst. told me to punch its lights out. bloody knuckles, bloody fist, bloody fish.

grabbed my pocket knife. gutted it from tail to chin. the good river carried the entrails and fins down to the sea lions and bull sharks.

washed the grime and scales off my hands in warm running ripples. took the catch to shore. wrapped it in a plastic walmart shopping bag.

got back out there. caught some more. by the time the sun went down, i must have tallied eight in total, but only kept one or two.

barroom cheers of approval, shouts of praise, still echoed in my ears hours after my final cast.

i started packing up my bait and tackle. and he corralled his twelve empty glass bottles.

sat down in the passenger seat of that little korean subcompact. reluctance, hesitation, fear. held onto the oh-shit handle as my drunk driver swerved us home.

thought about all the ways i could prepare my bony river bounty, if i made it back. tried to think about anything but the fact that i just might die in a cheap green kia on a curving country road.

focus on the passing cows, sheep, blueberry fields, grapevines, horses, and farmland. not a very long trip. but it felt like a million miles.

eighth grade funeral

tragic first period class.

homeroom full of rumors
and nauseous speculation.

somebody in our midst
lost something crucial.

counselors came in
bearing pastries, apology,
and whitewashed words.

we didn't understand.

it was a guilty screaming gut-
punch when she didn't return.

she's been in angel dirt
for about eleven years now.

she'll never grow up—
static, frozen, yet unforgettable.

yes, i still recall her slow dancing
in the darkened disco ball gym,
fielding my nervous stammering.

that's right, i also remember her
running over with her friends
to see my new aluminum crutches
at the friday night football game.

but the very last time i saw her
was at the locker bay after school.

she had only hours then.
no one knew that, not even her.

lexa taught us how fragile we were:

little wooden ticonderoga pencils
primed to snap, splinter,
and choke under pressure.

ashes

step onto the charter boat.
the earth below becomes uncertain.

hit the throttle.
leave behind that maritime town.

cut through murky yaquina bay.
all the way to rock island.

welcome the smell of faded fog.
residual salt clings to everything.

grasp whatever you can.
the vessel jumps from crest to trough.

watch eared seals loaf and sing.
their voices sound the death knell.

see the sun slice the waves.
he dives down under the green brine.

listen to the low moan of the buoy.
kill engine and birth anchor.

start playing an old song.
saunter toward the stern.

behold a layer of familiar dust.
it dances with roses on the surface.

say goodnight and goodbye.
tuck what remains into the seabed.

poet kills bird

a seventh-grade boychild plods around the backyard.

in his flowerbed periphery: a twitching, stuttering movement.

a mini chirper, either a sparrow or a bluebird.

petite from afar, though up close, puffed like a parrot pea.

trapping air under velveteen down, birdie was cold, birdie was in poor shape.

craven twelve-year-old hands held the tiny critter in noonday rays,

stroking its ethereal gossamer, its hollowed-out osseous parts.

how he tried to shake it back to its senses, to rouse it from its pained dying.

the light in there was waning, its eyes were in its head.

floating over to the woodshed, an ax materialized in the boy's grip.

strolling toward the suffering in earnest, the question hung above his crown.

but eventually, it came down, and found its answer.

little fella disappeared into a veil of feathers.

it was one hell of a euthanasia.

no undo button, no rewind: the tape's all eaten up.

a stradivarius out of tune, out of time, in potting soil splinters.

no shoebox nurse, no animal hospital.

only a syringe plunged, a glass bottle emptied.

just some jeweled remains in shallow earth, wings clipped in perpetuity.

he robbed something from the sky and put it in the ground forever.

from that day on, his feet never felt heavier.

until next time, buddy

i.
moose is having a seizure again. poor dog. grab a bag of white sugar and a
spoon. try to feed
him sweetness to extract, to sieve away the bitter pain. undo his collar.
console his stiff, tender
neck and tight, cramping muscles. saliva pools, dripping from stygian lips
onto shiny linoleum.
concern, panic, fear, sorrow—in those big puppy dog eyes—glistening with
saline. wait for the fit
to stop. give fragile reassurance. proffer hugs and kisses. pet the bridge of his
snout.
hold him as he swims through the peril.

ii.
moose:
was a fighter, undefeated—he went the distance.
caught mice, and hid them to avoid confiscation.
took credit for our cat's plume-covered prey.
slept at the foot of my bed, keeping winter toes warm.
patiently entertained my dizzy six-string fumblings.
was the color of dark tourmaline and chocolate.
a true pal when i didn't have any others.
my first friend, really, second to my brother.
would shun sticks and bones for a pack of grimmway farms.
picked the red bits out of his purina dinner.
ran rowdy laps around the house after a bath, little nails
click click clicking.
lasted about eleven years.

iii.
moose,
i miss you with all my heart.
i hope i can be with you someday, the dynamic duo once more.
i knew you from when i was a toddler until sophomore year.
i remember the day i met you, when you came from the pound,
when you were so small.
i don't know where you went, where you are, but
i'm glad you're no longer suffering from your robbing condition.

iv.
moose, to this day, i see your face in every passing pooch on the street.
i still have your dog tag, if ever you decide to come back.

maison de rêve

evil stays outside your walls. god's penal code isn't welcome. no one screams at you. nightmares are nonexistent. emotional barbed wire is cast out. you are allowed to be a child and experience wonderment. no one pretends to call the cops or santa. you don't need to turn up the tv to stop the shouting. anvils don't hang overhead. hands don't fly. secrets aren't kept. dishes aren't hurled. wait until your dad gets home isn't uttered. family is a happy word. wine, beer, and vodka are personae non gratae. dreaming is encouraged. your pets live forever. you never have to drive your parents back from the bar. punishment isn't given out like candy. belts are just for pants, not young bodies. your virgin heart knows no hate, and suffers no abuse here.

oakland 2011

850 blue steel barrels. crosshairs fixed on your forehead. notes dropped in lockers. unspeakable nicknames. sometimes anon. sometimes not so much. love, pimple mustache. xo. you said get me out of this no gas station for four miles village. shots fired in whistlestops soar. clipped birds are still birds. remember how your heart wings folded origami. halved and brittled. creased. like leather letterman arms. forced to play the game. what if you didn't catch that ball. coaches made a wager. they saw a lump in the endzone. hell, everyone did. a lump in shoulder pads. a lump in the library. a lump in the science lab. a lump learning god only helps lucky kids. please, you said no more no more no more. wishing every night. for someone to take you out of your life. for someone to say get in the car. i've come to save you babe. from your drunk kid dead kid nowhere. your damned rotgut town. your impossible to get out of town. buckle up. curves ahead.

gaggle

the hatchling
stands on tiptoes,
asking the silvermagic
bathroom mirror
when he'll be able
to trade gosling plumage
for a shiny new gander coat.

fearing that he'll look
like a child forever,
he keeps returning
to funhouse medicine cabinets,
angling triptych panel doors just right
in hopes of seeing hundreds of himself:

always wishing
to find a fully fledged face
somewhere in that crowd.

waking up one morning
twenty-something years on,
he washed his feathered visage,
and through another reflecting pool,
started to wonder if he could
conjure up that baby goose for a change,
desiring rewind instead of fast forward:

but there's nothing left—
his youthful imagination
dried up like a birdbath
on a sweltering mid-july day.

if only he could remember
how the world looked
when he was a lot closer to the ground.

armistice

i wonder how he's faring
    night after night in my closet.
        darkness reveals his lemonseed eyes,
        that dear serpentine stalker, my monster.
    perhaps he's a cousin to that watersnake
who curled up next to my body on warm bedrock.
the same one that slithered after me
    through the rushing waters of clear creek.
        i never did anything to him.
        i never asked for his fangs.
    i used to check under my bed
every night before i went to sleep.
but i never knew what i'd do
    if i found him there with a crooked smile.
        now i get beneath the sheets with abandon.
        he can take me if he wants me.
    i'm tired of running
from scaly skin and razor rattles.
maybe we're both tired of the chase,
    maybe we can make a truce.
        yes, tonight, we'll meet in the sun again,
        and shed our past as reptiles do.

static

acting the clown yet running out of spraying carnations; handkerchiefs; balloon animals.

wearing your marathon shoes, but finding yourself on a slow motion hamster wheel.

a heartbreak beyond hyperbole—it bares its teeth still.

trying your damnedest to get up in the morning, but you can't find your feet.

bad winters becoming bad springs, bad summers, and worse falls.

sexy bottles: curvy frosted figures that never give you enough love & always run out.

being chased by a snake in klamath headwaters.

searching for a god, praying, begging to audiences absent.

crying into your bunk bed pillow, because pencil people keep getting erased.

relapse after relapse, another recovery stunted.

doing your best laurie strode, living life in spite of your own michael myers.

pneumonia at 3 months then 9 years—e.r. saline drips are friendly faces to you.

eating the crumbs, ignorant of the loaf they fell from.

hostile chimpanzee smiles behind every door, every darkened corner.

feeling like a late night tv snowy sendoff: channel 3 without any rca cables plugged in.

lament

when you stopped
     looking at ladybugs

like they were miracles

     like they shouldn't be there

but they somehow were,

and you started looking
     at them like

i've seen
     a million of you before,

     that's the day you died.

that's the day you stopped
     loving yourself.

damaged parts, no warranty

his body has arms.
has legs. has cellulite.
has all the important
bits. an egg shaped,
oval headed skull.
thickened fear stowed
in pores and cells. a
necklace made of
blemishes. the kaput
countenance of a
tender artist. a small
gut bearing lightning
bolt stretch marks.
strange hairy skin.
yellowing teeth.
lopsided craven
stubble that won't
manifest into a beard.
his scars. his acne
battle wounds. his
puggish nose. his big
funny ears. his
ordinary brown eyes.
he hides his physique,
dressing in billowy
black and blue.
because he feels them
staring: the roving
bands of preachers;
the flies buzzing on a
picnic; the crooked
broken fingers
pointing; the cruel
laughter. makes him
want to just get in a
rocket ship and never
come back. maybe on
a distant planet the
aliens will think he's
beautiful. he hopes
the feeling's contagious.

don't take my word for it [bad advice]

cower from your gothic rockabilly mind.

be horrified by those judging, stranger stares.

hold it back when letting it out is all that counts.

be unwilling to disco dance on the blacktop.

push it all down.

stifle tears at the movies.

avoid getting cat hair on your clothes even if it means purring and whiskers.

fear the planes soaring overhead as if they're bearing nukes.

reject what meets your gaze in a stormy puddle's machinations.

be terrified to put your shoulders back and walk high as mountains do.

savage your senses.

deny that deep well of vulnerability, your soft white corpus must remain private.

scurry from thoughts left-of-the-dial.

be scared to speak velvet words.

second guess your burning cinnamon getup.

be reluctant to take your shirt off at the sandy beach.

shy away from ugly crying, retching, heaving in the shower. be ashamed to ask for a hug.

put your feelings on layaway.

be afraid to care.

be so hard.

s.o.s.

samsara makes
all the same thoughts
circle like a prayer wheel
in my skull, brain, gut,
shaking a brittle birch
with paper leaf flutter.
little hopes drifted away
when i answered that question.
i came to seek help.
is it a disorder?
those monkeys won't get off.
trauma keeps me where
i don't want to be.
stuck in shuffling
daydreams of suffering
and foreboding pain.
the heart slaps
the hand that rocks; the cradle
tipped over and the baby's head
caved in, filled by emptiness,
abuse, words, dark nothings.
siddhartha steps out
of comfortable clothes
to join the samanas.
he wants to stop
the self hatred, self contempt,
shame of his life, his body,
and his soul:
how sick it is sometimes.
how well he knows it could be.

a sudden shift in glasnost

i sent my sexual shadow to a siberian gulag. half of my soul was kept from the precious light. no one really knew her, not even me. i feared the hammer, i feared the sickle. i was scared of what they'd call us, so i squashed her with my boot heels. i threw my friend into the polar wastelands. but across any etcetera, there she was, after all i put her through. always urging me to pay heed to the portents, to look inward. pleading with me to listen, or else face the buzzsaw of self denial. both of us grew tired of the charade, the stupid disguises, the iron curtain: pretending i don't like boys too. somehow she's forgiven me. ever since i let her out, we walk hand in hand, in step with each other. i can't escape her, and i wouldn't want to. we're a federation of one, reunited at last.

j. dean boys

it's not like the teen rebel movies / you find the black bookbag / take out the pens and paper / replace em with socks / clean underwear / do i take my toothbrush / will the seats lay back that far / what if someone finds me / like a roly poly / in slumber / the windows ain't tinted / think of it as a sleepover / in the high school parking lot / right next to ballfield fences / what if i get caught / is this just a mayday / to see if anybody still cares / the cops never helped me before / why would they now / the smalltown gossip engine / turns over again / is this bad / am i bad / am i apple / am i rotten / when the neighborhood hears / will they kill the boy / or just scare him / thwarted boys / scorned boys / remember / the wimpy boys / boys with no balls / jailbreak boys / boys with no fucking guts / boys that got walked over / them was me / and me was them / boys are evolving / new organs to digest grief / boys in floor length mirrors / size themselves up / left hook / right uppercut / just in case / boys like me danced / like i was in the ring / boy me cried / like i gave a damn / readied myself / for domestic enemies / was i a good boy then / am i a good boy now / boy i can't imagine / putting another boy through it / never / i refuse / will i ever be daddy / do i want boys / i don't / no / i'll never make boys / seriously ponder / spending the night / as runaways / like i did / never boys / need never desert / never boys / need never ask / will the white boat car start / is there gas in the tank / will i be warm tonight / in my flannel sleeping bag / will it keep me safe / will i die here / will i die without / a boy kiss / a girl kiss / a kiss kiss /

fairy tale

i was a girl last night. sawing wood. après-xy.
i embodied elegance—more harp, less banjo.
less celluloid, more silver screen.
felt like i was slipping into some delicate,
provocative satin number.
cascading rivers of black piano keys rested easy
on my graceful shoulders. plucked a handful,
put it behind my ears.
an honest smile arrived. crossed my legs,
looked at my countenance, and blushed.
my face was moleskin-soft, but had sort of a
red delicious hue. a bit of pink lady, too.
freckles vaulted across my nose. forming a
peace bridge, a peace arch—a ceasefire adopted.
been at war with myself for too long.
my jawline became more forgiving, extra
supple. i lost all my godforsaken chin stubble,
forgetting all about that beesting aftershave.
i was a tender, powerful dropout.
welling, deep, doe eyes glistened in the light.
they had the spark of life in there, couldn't be
extinguished by anything.
not some raggedy ann facsimile. not a centerfold
either. simply, purely, woman.
juster, fairer, paler. no adam's apple to be seen.
i was a hopeful, longing, amorous ingénue.
so imagine my devastation. picture my let-down,
my disappointment, when the alarm crowed out
cock-a-doodle-doo.

awaken

 *up on the sloping diving board,
plunging into that heaven
i've been told to avoid
my entire [repressed] life.
 *his body: a warm, crackling fire,
a soft climax, a safety blanket
wrapped around my limbs.
 *unlike those other guilty nights,
i embraced it all for a change.
 *of all my tormented moments
of confused crisis, this one was nirvana,
was total abandon, was completely right.
 *yes, it felt natural running my hands
up his thighs, with fingers stroking to taste.
 *genuine attraction without the asterisk,
these are the latent kisses
i've wanted to land for years.
 *i'm not drowning down here—
this is no pool of tears, i can swim after all.
 *that lifeguard can go home early,
i'm tired of hiding my dazzling fins.

i wrote your name at the top of the neues rathaus

blown away. i was a smoke ring from your sherlock bowl. yeah, nine months felt long and short. a patchwork history. woven with firsts. now, it's far gone. a story in shards. a busted hellenic vase. anyways, i'm sorry i trashed that hat box. full of mementos freely given. national forest gems. disposable camera shots of you and me. all those tchotchkes. coffee mugs, books, letters, skipping stones. they're sitting in a landfill somewhere. ozymandias monuments to lost love. my door was covered with our faces. but in time, i took us down. an entrance morphed into an exit. once, it was all a rush to the head. once, we were kids. growing up together. pulled under by a maelstrom of novelty. sometimes i miss that drowning feeling. sometimes i miss you.

beach street

decades passed, &
a castle once blue
faded to skeleton gray:
bits of bone chipped and
floated away in snowflakes,
covering us with lead paint.
today, corpse wood still sags
from a bulging ceiling well
we put kitchen pans under,
depending on phone forecasts:
them dripping droppings
never stopped and
neither did that mold.
even so, let me catch
my own dog days with a
hippocampus bucket, & i'll
keep them till i'm drained,
on some sunny morn foretold.
            i miss my old buddy.
used to see him on the couch
but now we only text
ever since the move in may.
want to tell him all about
my new favorite bands, yet
i know he's already heard
those midwest emo songs
from that s. oregon bedroom,
and so have his rafters, the
plaster, torn linoleum, and
arrhythmic washer/dryer.
my current mattress,
skin, face, and lungs
are the same i had then.
but here at this address
i need not dodge
ants, splinters, or anything
except for city noise.
still, it would be nice
to spend another night there,
the charming punk home
with the lovely rat hazards.
            sincerely: pining for then.

we held hands

like rigored mannequins. skipping across denver ave. singing salad days are now. there we were. two feral kids. sharing a pack of coffin nails. under a 31 foot tall statue of paul bunyan. seeking refuge. lazing on median grass. everything was consecrated. seeing god himself would have won silver. that night was golden. yet, gazing up into the woodsman's lonesome blinkers, something felt shanghaied. dustdeviled away. hurricaned away. so we decided to ask him a question: do you love, giant? at once, in a heavy mainer accent: i only ever loved one lady, but she quit me. our lumberjack reached down to bum a dart, leaving us with this: we all deserve a vice or two, they never leave you. we said farewell colossus. followed by a whispered prayer. for him & his long lost ox. that night, you saw me home. and called in the morning. to make sure i was still there.

better med

escitalopram:
strike a lunar stance for me.
i hope you taste of lemon lime,
soda, and gumdrops.
candy comatose
used to make us higher
than any drug we can find now
in liquor stores, dispensaries,
or pharmacopeia indexes.
with any luck, you won't
make me sick like too much
sugar on halloween;
the morning after a battle
with a case of blended scotch;
a head full of demon thoughts.
instead, free me like the helpless,
spinning critter you once caught
hanging from your ceiling:
trap me in a drinking glass
and carefully, sweetly,
set me down on the stairs.

highway 62

i hope that rocky bridge is still there.

i hope the waterfall still rushes
and that creek up union way still runs.

i hope the huckleberries are forever in season
to make those pies for becky:

and to keep a traveler's mind pointed homeward.

i hope i'd know the way there,
even if the roads were all washed out.

i hope i can find my own way,
road signs and pavement be damned.

roll on tanner creek

goodnight sun. everything's starting to look like dinosaur bones. bowl
sparked visions of one too many bacchanals. it's your favorite hour. all
the watering holes are closed and the queens already took their wigs off.
puffing periques in the closet when you swore you were alone. that early
a.m. inspiration guiding your lips to say another night in the bag. impish
murmurs inviting you to a moondance. along custard yellow streetlamped
streets. you belong to the folks who write verse on bathroom blackboards.
those who scratch their names into mirrors & toilet seats with house keys.
you're graffiti's biggest fan. you're the reason ethel leaves slip covers on
her furniture and keeps her good dinnerware locked up. believed i was the
last libertine, reciting taoist tenets out loud; getting ode to a ruffian tatted
on my thigh; tap dancing with fluffy cat tail shoes. but sitting at the bus
stop today, i heard someone cry aww as you kissed me on the cheek. and
looking at you, i thought to myself, oh how i love people just like that.

now i know why tom & huck staged their own funerals

got me a mansion of selves bottled up inside. they're having roommate disagreements about libertad again. the palace is on fire. can't do nothin to quell the burning. cause i'm mired in the hell called i. need detention from myself. need hermitage from myself. necesito una separación from myself. asylum from myself. desert island from myself. i wear long hair, denim ball caps, taiwan manufactured wayfarers—in hopes of fading in to the fullest extent. i'm a mortar at the county fireworks show. climb to fall. apex to peak. alpha to omega. then start anew. please excuse me, i'm a firefighter, but not by trade or pleasure. i keep putting seasoned madrone on my jack flash coalbed. that is, until the flames die, and i get what i always wanted: to live life in a vacuum. no one will know me. just like that first coat of paint on aunt polly's white picket fence. olvidado.

au revoir

if a meteor
or a stray bullet
comes down
and paints the day
with my hot love:
look upon the
wondrous bloody
scarlet sidewalk,
and admire
my final work.

if i become
a hit & run statistic,
flattened by a big bus,
truck, or speeding car,
by drivers distracted
behind the wheel:
then keep an eye out
for this handsome face
on the 6:00 news.

if i die of a tumor,
a subcutaneous stowaway,
unseen, unfelt, undetected:
don't blame the little guy,
for he was just doing his job.

if my mind and body
file divorce papers
sooner than expected:
i'll laugh
with my last
rattling breath,
knowing i got out
while there was still
water to drink.